WEST HIGHLAND

LANDSCAPE

First published in Great Britain by
Colin Baxter Photography Ltd.,
Unit 2/3, Block 6, Caldwellside Industrial Estate,
LANARK, ML11 6SR

British Library Cataloguing in Publication Data
Baxter, Colin
  West Highland Landscape.
  1. Scotland. Western highlands. Description & travel
  I. Title II. Crumley, Jim
  914.11'804858

  ISBN 0-948661-04-6

Front Cover Photograph Eilean Donan Castle
Back Cover Photograph Beinn Damph and Loch Torridon

Printed in Great Britain by Frank Peters (Printers) Ltd., Kendal

WEST HIGHLAND
LANDSCAPE

PHOTOGRAPHS BY COLIN BAXTER

WITH TEXT BY JIM CRUMLEY

COLIN BAXTER PHOTOGRAPHY LTD., LANARK.

INTRODUCTION

POSTCARDS ARE an irresistible response to the West Highlands of Scotland . . . a fistful of favourite views, a few scribbled words of greeting to convey something of the surroundings to well-chosen friends. Rubbing shoulders with such a succession of landscapes is an experience which nourishes a compulsive urge to share their sensations.

This book is a kind of elaborate postcard . . . a portfolio of photographs which set out to ensnare the landscape's most captivating moods; a collection of essays which seek out something of the essence of those landscapes as they unfold, engulf, recede. Like all long-suffering travellers in the West Highlands, we have our preferences — favourite places, favourite seasons, favourite reasons for being there. We have lingered unashamedly over these, so this collaboration of our journeyings northwards from Rannoch Moor to Sutherland is a particularly subjective memento, but surely that is in the best postcard tradition.

Colin Baxter
Jim Crumley

July 1989

". . . a subjective memento" of the West Highlands . . .

"We have lingered unashamedly over our preferences . . ." Loch Alsh *(above)* and Torridon *(facing)*.

"Rain effects a curious tension about Glencoe's close-gathered walls . . ."

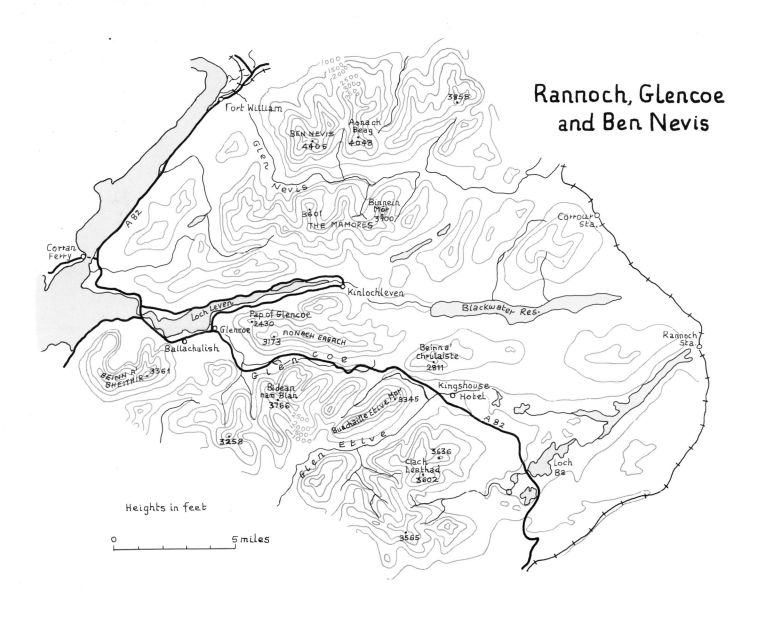

Rannoch, Glencoe
and Ben Nevis

Fort William

Glen Nevis

BEN NEVIS
4406

Aonach
Beag
4048

·3858

Binnein
Mor
·3700

·3601
THE MAMORES

Corrour
Sta.

A 82

Corran
Ferry

Kinlochleven

Blackwater Res.

Loch Leven

Pap of Glencoe
·2430

Glencoe

AONACH EAGACH
3173

Rannoch
Sta.

Beinn a'
chrulaiste
·2811

Ballachulish

BEINN A'
BHEITHIR ·3361

Glencoe

Bidean
nam Bian
·3766

Kingshouse
Hotel

Buachaille Etive Mor
·3345

·3258

2500
3000

Glen   Etive

A 82

·3636

Clach
Leathad
·3602

Loch
Ba

Heights in feet

0   5 miles

·3585

RANNOCH, GLENCOE AND BEN NEVIS

It is a different land beyond Rannoch. However you encounter that high, primitive moor, you will leave it looking askance over your shoulder.

Its prospect from the Glencoe road has presence enough to infiltrate even such impenetrables as the glass of a tour coach, the cocoon of a car. The train floats deftly across its eastern margins (its track sustained by a technique so technologically logical it was invented by the Romans), pausing at two of the unlikliest stations in the Highlands, brushing the tawny flanks of untroubled deer, threading teeming waters on scraps of land. The memory of the Moor's traverse on foot will last a lifetime, recurring sharp as frosted grass in any personal retrospective of wilderness days, long after the detail of mountain jaunts have fudged and fogged. There are so many mountains in this kingdom of the west; there is just the one Rannoch Moor.

It is whiles an uneasy place well-strewn with treacheries. Neil Munro read it well in "The New Road": his assessment still holds good.

"Eastward, where the inn front looked, the moor stretched flat and naked as a Sound; three days' march from end to end they said were on it — all untracked and desert-melancholy . . . God-forgotten, man-forsworn, wild Rannoch,

"The memory of the Moor's traverse will last a lifetime . . ."

11

"The Moor is a sea of many mountain shores"

with the birds above it screaming, was the oddest thing, the eeriest in nature he had ever seen. It charmed and repelled him . . .

"Half a dozen times before the noon that day, he walked up to the brae from which the moor was widest seen, and looked across it with uneasy breast, and drank, as one might say, the spirit of the wilderness, so strange and so forlorn . . ."

The Moor is still a reservoir of that spirit, feeding lands beyond, clinging to the treads of travellers like thistledown on the flanks of sheep, so that the travellers as they journey ever north, ever west, scatter the seeds of the spirit and so perpetuate wilderness. Centuries of travellers with many motives have dusted the West Highland landscape with the wild spores of Rannoch Moor.

The Moor is a sea of many mountain shores. None is as unprepossessing as Beinn a'Chrulaiste, a blunt and bulky hill, a thing more of Sutherland than Argyll for its individualistic isolation slumped over the Moor's north-west corner; none is as commanding as Buachaille Etive Mor, "The Boochle" to every Scots hill gangrel who ever was, is a diamond among mountains, a landscape lynchpin which stops all manner of convoys in their westering tracks by the jaws of the Pass of Glencoe. Rockhounds and rock-bottom dawdlers find riches here.

So the Buachaille outshines, outclasses Beinn a'Chrulaiste across the road in every respect but one — it is the summit view from the unsung ben which spreadeagles the incomparable mountain, the incomparable moor and the

Buachaille Etive Mor: ". . . a landscape lynchpin by the jaws of the Pass of Glencoe"

Glencoe: ". . . a conducive arena for the conjuring of old bloodsheds"

incomparable glen, and establishes that unique perspective which delineates the beginning and the end and the frontier of the West Highlands. It IS a different land beyond Rannoch.

To win that land beyond, clear through to Sutherland, is this book's journey, to which end it must first dare the best-loved and best-reviled glen in all the Highlands and all their histories. Glencoe.

"The Glen of Weeping" is now a discredited, fanciful translation of Glencoe's Gaelic origins, but research has only taught what the name does not mean, for the true derivation is long obscured. For all that, the landscape still weeps; rain effects a curious tension about this glen's close-gathered walls, and it rains here at the least excuse.

There is, too, the old salt-eyed stain of the Massacre of 1692 which it seems must forever darken the name of Campbell. For all the atrocities in the repertoire of man's inhumanities to man long forgotten before and since, the Massacre of Glencoe still offends, not just Macdonalds, but millions of neutrals the world over. Facts merely confuse. It was just one outrage in an era which thrived on outrage; it was an appalling botch of a massacre in which only 38 died and 300 escaped. Perhaps, as many contend, its notoriety lingers and rankles still because the principle of Highland hospitality was abused. Perhaps. Rather, I believe that the Glencoe landscape is a brooding preservative, a conducive arena for the conjuring of old bloodsheds. If it had all happened on bright, wind-rinsed Ardnamurchan, it would be but a footnote to history, and not a claim to infamy.

"Rock-hounds and rock-bottom dawdlers find riches here"

The mountains are as mesmeric as they have always been, however, whether you stand and stare or climb to look them in the eye. From the crown of Glencoe, Bidean nam Bian, the Highlands loll away and away in every direction, most compellingly northwards and westwards to far seas. Yet even from that singular summit, and in all the tumbledown, rutted, snow-hewn scheme of mountainous things, one massive shape overwhelms the northern horizon. From any direction, from any distance, there is no mistaking the one we call simply "The Ben".

Uniquely among Scottish mountains, Ben Nevis is undiminished by distance. Even the Cairngorms look almost benign from afar. The Ben, so often horn-locked with its own storm, so contemptuous of human life at every level of mountaineering competence, has never learned to effect even the illusion of meekness. From 50 miles or 50 yards, it commands immensely. Its impact on both the landscape and the minds of men has spawned a long and distinguished literature which shows no sign of abating. The most recent contribution, "Ben Nevis, Britain's Highest Mountain" — by climber Ken Crocket, is among the best, charting 400 years of man's often fatal fascination for the mountain.

That the fascination is far from unanimously affectionate, however, is reflected in these lines from mountaineer-poet Hamish Brown's startingly unflattering tribute. "The Harlot" has appeared many times in many publications, notably Hamish's own collection "Time Gentlemen":

Yet it is to this harlot
the generations come — brash boys
to test their nascent lusts,
a giggle that so often has an echoed death.

I have come to hate the bitch.

The sterile heart of her is stone
and her smile is slimy ice.
We should have heeded the old advice:
not all snowy frills — or hills — are nice.

The brash boys still fall for her all the same, and many never learn immunity to her seductions in a lifetime. Thousands who never climbed another hill and never will stumble up as much of the pony track as they can thole. To stand on the summit of Scotland is Everest enough for them, and if you catch her in rare benevolent mood, even a harlot has charms.

Ben Nevis: "From any distance, there is no mistaking the one we call simply 'The Ben' . . ."

Ardnamurchan: ". . . more an island with a land bridge than a peninsula"

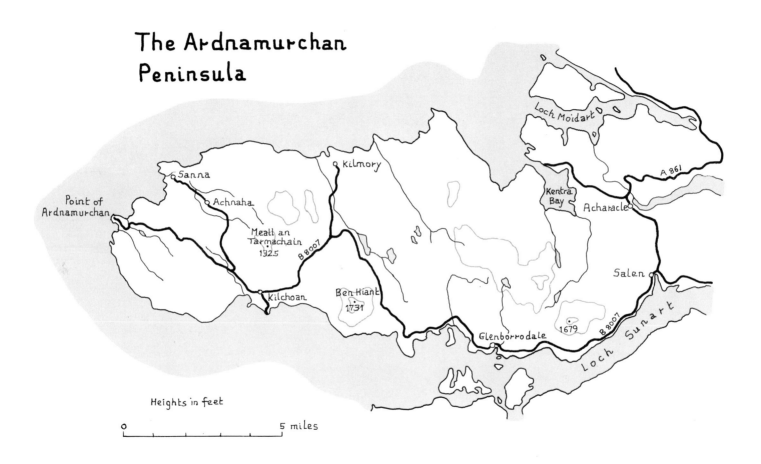

The Ardnamurchan Peninsula

Loch Moidart

A 861

Kentra Bay

Acharacle

Sanna

Kilmory

Achnaha

Point of Ardnamurchan

Meall an Tarmachain 1325

B 8007

Salen

Kilchoan

Ben Hiant 1731

1679

B 8007

Glenborrodale

Loch Sunart

Heights in feet

0   5 miles

THE ARDNAMURCHAN PENINSULA

Ardnamurchan is more Hebridean than West Highland, more an island with a land-bridge than a peninsula. Even now, it takes a tortuous circuit to achieve the land-bridge's crossing, and the Corran Ferry across Loch Linnhe is still Ardnamurchan's best-used, best-loved portal, the last surviving mainland-to-mainland ferry in the Highlands.

The shores of Loch Linnhe's narrows are chalk and fragrant cheese, the east burdened with the loud and sprawling implications of Fort William and the trade-and-tourist routes north; the west a sparsely-tramped, sea-glittered, oak-dusted way which dwines and dawdles to the edge of the sunset. By the time you have threaded that lesser road to its ocean, you are as far west as Stornoway, further west than much of Mull, all of Eigg or the Cuillins. The mainland of Scotland goes no further west than this.

So for those thirled to Ardnamurchan, whether by birth or by its luring landscape, the Corran Ferry's crabwise gait is imbued with a heavy significance. Alasdair Maclean, poet of Ardnamurchan, whose "Night Falls on Ardnamurchan" is a well-crafted milestone in the literature of the West, calls it "a kind of mobile decompression chamber where various kinds of pollution were drained from the blood and I was fitted to breathe pure air again."

"Hebridean associations are irresistible"

"It is winter for the oakwoods ..."

Despite the implied slur on the good air of North Argyll, it is not such a fanciful analogy, for Ardnamurchan is a place set aside, still wilder than much of the West Highlands, and the ultimate preserve of those who seek the unique peaces of the cul-de-sac.

The road dives decisively west at Salen into a landscape so seemingly green and wooded that it might be Mull or south Skye — Hebridean associations are irresistible. Roads on Ardnamurchan are forever diving, and almost invariably they dive down variations on a theme of west, for west is the only serious journey the roadmakers ever countenanced here. Half-hearted tributaries traipse north and south to and from that thrusting mainstream, short-lived divings to such as machair-stained Sanna, ancient Kilmory, volcano-girdled Achnaha, far-flung stoical townships with salt on their breath, poised it seems in the perpetual patient shruggery of the sea-besieged and the history-beleaguered.

Rock-ribbed brown moors pile behind, a second-tiered shrug evoking the darkest frown of Harris. There are many island shades the length of this reluctant mainland.

The woods, of which the oakwoods are the dearest and Highland-rarest, are a deceiving, coast-hugging, burn-clinging throwback, an echo of the landscape that was. The richness of their meagre thrivings only underpins the sadness of the few moor-stragglers about their fringes, isolated trees you can set eerily against a sea-rooted ground mist in autumn dawns. It is winter for the oakwoods, however, for these are the last of their tribe.

Forge into the heart of the peninsula at Glenmore and the

"Ardnamurchan is still a place set aside, still wilder than much of the West Highlands"

"There are many island shades the length of this reluctant mainland"

high lochan-stained moors gather about them hills with names like Beinn na Mointich Leathainn, Hill of the Broad Moss, which is a fair enough account of the way the land lies. The nomenclature of old Gaeldom very often is, but whiles it is overtaken by events, natural and otherwise, and stranded as conspicuously ill-at-ease as a beached whale. It is a long time since ptarmigan worked their stone-still sorceries on the summit of Meall an Tarmachain. Ardnamurchan does not feature in any new assessment of the domain of ptarmigan; they have long since withdrawn eastward and upward.

Nothing the crouching hills of Mull can offer spares Ardnamurchan the onslaughts of the Atlantic and its teeming weathers.

To lean into the furies of an Iceland-bound hurricane's shore-swiping tail on the rocks of Briaghlann is to be humbled by unfettered energy, raw and primitive and unstoppable. The sky falls on the ocean black as night, the sea drains of all colour but gray and white, enraged winds slice lumps from the queueing corrugations of waves, and Ardnamurchan's most famous focal point, the lighthouse, blurs as the smashed sea leaps for the throat of the banshee.

In the frantic midst of all that, two cormorants ride the boiling ocean wearing the unperturbed demeanour of creatures in their element. There is no point in flying such seas, so sit on them. They have seen all this before and know their immunity. Not so the rock pipits and the curlews. They shelter on a leeward ledge, storm-stymed, while two whooper swans, advance guard of the Iceland hordes, hug the frail seaward shore of Loch Grigadale, gasping, it seems, for

breath. It is a long trek down the northern ocean for such a landfall.

In half a day the thing is done. A flood here, a slain birch there, a white-weeping hillside . . . these are its legacy. Ardnamurchan re-emerges as the rains suddenly stutter and soften through warm winds and rainbows into a glittering, born-again evening. Every cottage storm-porch reeks of dripping Barbours and oilskins and by nightfall the star millions have overwhelmed the hurricane-bowed sky. Through all the moonlit hours, Ardnamurchan's mountain masterpiece, Ben Hiant, runs white with waterfalls which will be still by dawn. That new day's passenger cargo over Corran will find the place enchanted and wonder at the fuss the natives make of the weather.

"The ultimate preserve of those who seek the unique peaces of the cul-de-sac"

The Five Sisters of Kintail: ". . . liberally peaked like erratic battlements . . ."

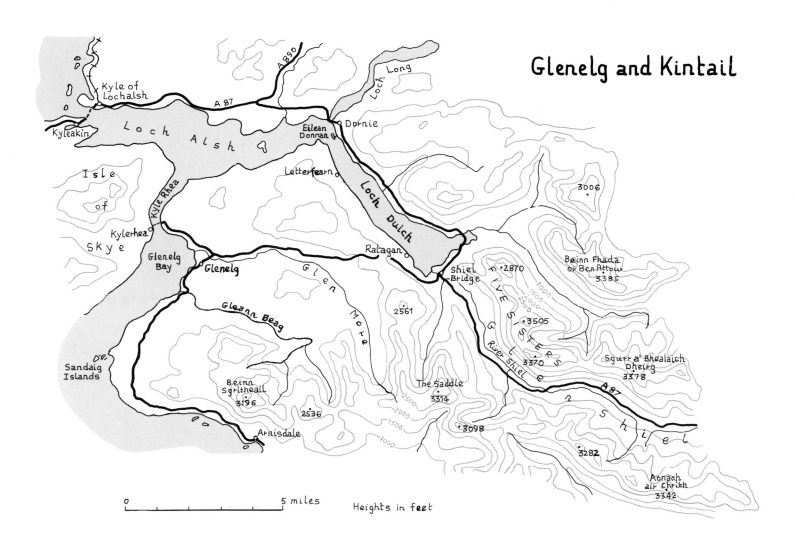

Glenelg and Kintail

Kyle of Lochalsh

A 87

A 890

Loch Long

Kyleakin

Loch Alsh

Eilean Donnan

Dornie

Isle

of

Kyle Rhea

Letterfearn

Loch Duich

3006

Skye

Kylerhea

Glenelg Bay

Glenelg

Ratagan

Shiel Bridge

•2870

Beinn Fhada or Ben Attow 3385

Glen More

Gleann Beag

2561

FIVE SISTERS

•3505

1500

1000

2500

River Shiel

•3370

Squrr a' Bhealaich Dheirg 3378

Sandaig Islands

Beinn Sgritheall 3196

2536

The Saddle 3314

Glen

Shiel

A 87

2500

2000

1500

1000

•3098

•3282

Aonach air Chrith 3342

Arnisdale

0   5 miles

Heights in feet

GLENELG
AND KINTAIL

Deep under Beinn Sgritheall, fended off by the devilments of the Wade Road over Mam Rattagan, wrapped in the impenetrables of an unconfiding Commission forest, a modest track cramps dimly down to a shelf of turf, a swirl of shingle, a small skein of islands, the silvered Sound of Sleat, the matchless proximity of Skye.

The song of that place is a waterfall, its dance a burn which pales and curves and glitters in a wide arc to the sea. Kathleen Raine, poet, ensnared its essence in a form of words which would travel the world, albeit in someone else's book.

"He has married me with a ring, a ring of bright water . . ."
Gavin Maxwell lived here.

He called it Camusfearna, and through the story of his life and his otters, unfurled a literature of the land which Scotland is perhaps still too slow to acknowledge. Reality is Sandaig, and for a fervent handful of the millions whose lives Maxwell touched with his books, a place of discreet pilgrimage. Twenty years after his death, 30 years after Ring of Bright Water, they come still.

It is a captivating shore, wild with birds, brushed by wakes of countless sea creatures, drenched by the autumn anthems of stags. It is the quiet footnote to the four-season presidency of Beinn Sgritheall which spills Maxwell's burn — the Allt Mor Shantaig — from a cold womb in its summit rocks,

". . . the matchless proximity of Skye"

33

3196 swift feet above the waterfall. Man and otter are remembered here. A rock where the house stood covers Maxwell's ashes; a cairn by the burn echoes the dedication in "Raven Seek Thy Brother" to his otter, Edal: "Whatever joy you had from her, give back to nature".

Edal died in 1968 in the fire which destroyed Maxwell's home. The following year, he too was dead, but something of him survives here almost tangibly. Whatever the tragedies and shortcomings of his flawed life, this landscape was his saving grace. He in turn was its glad ambassador and in the literature it spawned were his finest hours.

Beinn Sgritheall is a mountain of many waters, most of which are summoned to the Gleann Beag River, where they gather darkly for Glenelg Bay, a small headland or two north of Sandaig. Gleann Beag is unexceptional by the standards of its surroundings, douce and green in its lower reaches, wildering only as it starts to climb east among the flanks of the mighty Saddle and the heartland of Kintail. First, it unveils two ancient stone fragments, contemporaries of Christ, which are nothing less than the foundation stones of Scottish architecture itself: the Gleann Beag brochs.

Dun Telve and Dun Troddan are the finest of their ancient stone tribe to be found anywhere on the Scottish mainland (and outshone only in Orkney and Shetland), and Dun Telve, particularly, demonstrates the genius behind their intuitive architecture. Stewart Cruden's book, "The Scottish Castle", pays them this tribute:

"The origin of the style is wholly constructional, and the style so arresting as to imply a preconceived notion. It was an idea before it was a fact — the idea of a highly original mind . . . the most remarkable ancient castle in Europe." That mind, whoever flexed it, addressed itself exclusively to Scotland. The brochs are nowhere else. Ian Hannah, in "The Story of Scotland in Stone" wrote of them as "those earliest buildings of any note that press our rock-bound soil. Nothing very like them has been found in any other land, and it is at least possible that they influenced our castles till the days of Mary Queen of Scots."

Their stamp, therefore, would be on everyone's favourite fortress of Kintail, and one of the most famous anywhere, although Eilean Donan Castle's chocolate box appeal is scarcely a fit tribute to the gore and lore which have fashioned its destiny. It remains, however, the most irresistible of buildings, the most admired, the most painted, the most photographed — irresistible still to every shade of photographic sophistication from box Brownie to Baxter.

Eilean Donan Castle, where the waters of Loch Duich, Loch Long and Loch Alsh comingle, is so unerringly sited, so confidently fashioned, that it has evolved over 700 years to stand as rooted in its landscape as the folded hills of Kintail or the skyline-scrolled Cuillins. It is a classic Scottish tower house whose long exile of dereliction ended in 1932 when its restoration was completed. It was rebuilt to the precise detail of the original with the assistance of a vision by one Farquhar MacRae of Auchtertyre. There are many who will baulk at accepting such an explanation at face value, but there are many uncanny components in the architecture of the Celtic character. The evidence is the manner in which

"The devilments of the Wade Road over Mam Rattagan" descend to Glenelg

Loch Alsh and "the sky-scrolled Cuillins"

that which was ruinous has been rebuilt, and the detail confirmed by old Edinburgh records.

Eilean Donan has been the domain of MacRaes, bodyguards to the MacKenzie chiefs of Kintail for more than 400 years. It is fitting enough that through that lineage this singular fortress has won the long and lasting peace it now enjoys.

If Eilean Donan Castle and the brochs are man's masterpiece in Kintail, Glen Shiel is nature's. Brenda Macrow's long-revered book "Kintail Scrapbook" calls it "The loveliest glen in the West Highlands", and neither the added girth of the road since then, nor its traffic, have damaged that assessment.

Mountains cram its airspace on both sides, a mightier landscape than Glencoe, and though battles and dark deeds were fought and fashioned here too, there is none of the Coe's melancholy, nor for that matter its notoriety. Glen Shiel is a bright, beautiful and majestic glen, as befits the first thoroughfare of bright, beautiful and majestic Kintail. Long, daunting ridges, liberally peaked like erratic battlements, scroll both sides of the glen, their prospects played west over Glenelg and Skye and Rhum, south into wildest Knoydart, east and north over a perpetually receding mountain land necklaced with lochs and their doodling rivers which knows no easy fertile respite this side of Orkney.

It is here in the heart of Kintail that a key turns, a door opens, and something of the hidden soul of the West Highlands is bared.

Eilean Donan Castle: ". . . everyone's favourite fortress of Kintail . . ."

"It is in Kintail that something of the hidden soul of the West Highlands is bared"

The benign seaward aspect of Loch Torridon

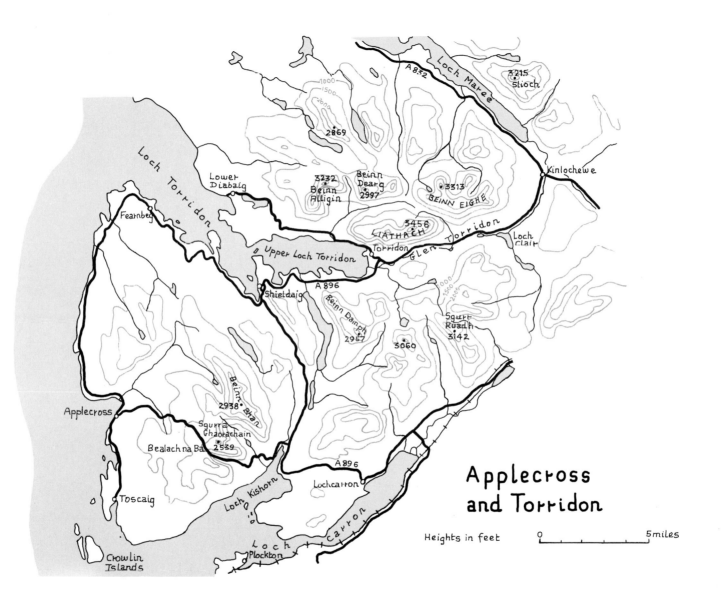

Loch Maree
A 832
3215 Slioch
Kinlochewe
1000
1500
2000
2869
Lower Diabaig
Loch Torridon
3232 Beinn Alligin
Beinn Dearg 2997
3313
BEINN EIGHE
Fearnbeg
3456
LIATHACH
Loch Clair
Torridon
Glen Torridon
Upper Loch Torridon
A 896
Shieldaig
Beinn Damph 2957
Squrr Ruadh 3142
3060
1500
1000
Beinn Bhan
2938
Applecross
Squrra Ghaobachain
Bealach na Ba 2539
A 896
Lochcarron
Toscaig
Loch Kishorn
Carron
Crowlin Islands
Loch
Plockton

Applecross and Torridon

Heights in feet   0   5 miles

APPLECROSS
AND TORRIDON

It is a bewilderment of watersheets which gathers and disperses about the headland of Balmacara. If you are threading the land rather than the water, you have just negotiated Loch Duich, Loch Long, Loch Alsh (with a glance down Kyle Rhea where Skye and the mainland lean closest); ahead, to left, right and centre, the Inner Sound, Loch Carron and Loch Kishorn interlock and interweave their currents and splay their salt fingers deep inland to taint the sweet, eager press of the hill burns and their swollen rivers for the sea.

Such is the seaward spell of Skye and Raasay in all this and the play of their suns and shadows and shifting storms, that Plockton creeps up on you with a faintly disconcerting dislocation of your sense of direction. Then you unravel the simple trick of the place, which is that it turns a shrugged back on the West, but by virtue of its broad gaze across Loch Carron, still contrives an illusion of facing seaward.

Plockton is a hale village, sound in architectural wind and limb. The place talks to you in a stone-and-slate speech which is as indigenous to the West as Gaelic.

Charles Rennie Mackintosh put a pricelessness on the Scottish architectural tradition . . . "the architecture of our own country, just as much Scotch as we are ourselves —

Shades of Applecross: Ardban *(facing)* **and Loch Kishorn** *(above)*

43

Glamaig on Skye from the Bealach na Ba

as indigenous as our wild flowers, our family names, our customs or our political constitutions".

The further north you journey in the West Highlands, the more conscious you become of the worth of an architecture which defers to its landscape. Where the tradition is most loyally honoured, it fits its landscape as surely as an old pinewood. Like the pinewoods, however, it is often a fragmentary allegiance you encounter so that you yearn for more stone and slate and small sash-and-case windows as you yearn for more pinewoods.

If you would now win over to Applecross, the road diverts you mightily and tortuously round Carron and Kishorn, and without so much as a "this road can damage your health" Government warning, fingerposts you west from Tornapress over the frothing Russel Burn on Scotland's last great motoring adventure, the Bealach na Ba. In good weather (with which Applecross is ungenerous), the gradients, the hairpins and the 2000ft summit make for an uneasily memorable trip to the seaside. In winter the journey is a lottery, and the long but lovely coastal miles of new road by Fearnbeg to Shieldaig offers Applecross's four-season dwellers a welcome if tortuous escape hatch. Brenda Macrow's vivid account in "Torridon Highlands" of catching the Stornaway-Kyle of Lochalsh steamer at Applecross by being rowed through a stormy sea for three miles at 4 a.m. serves to remind just how primitive communications with this part of the world remained until comfortably within the living memory of most of us.

What you may well miss as you grapple with the road are the scarred and scoured and serried corries of Beinn Bhan and

Shieldaig and "the oldest rock kingdom in the land . . ."

"Torridon's impact on the unwary is often an unnerving one"

Sgurr a' Ghaorachain, which are not only awesome on the eye and devilish to climb, but also signal your entry into the oldest rock kingdom in the land, and one of the oldest anywhere in the world.

Somewhere around 1000 million years ago, the rivers of some long-obliterated northern continent heaped their debris with a casual aggression onto a bedrock which was already perhaps 2000 million years old. When the science of geology was invented, it christened the bedrock Lewisian gneiss and the debris Torridonian sandstone. The sandstone, improbable as it now appears, has whittled down the eons to the stumps of once-upon-a-times, leaving those grimly impressive mountain sculptures of Torridon and their airier northern kin of West Sutherland. The permanence we fondly confer upon our mountains is no such thing, but here of all places their impermanence is a little more enduring than our own. It has always seemed worth pausing at the foot of the Bealach na Ba to pay homage and make what peace you can with the company you are about to keep.

The alternative to all this dire challenging of Applecross's landward frontiers is to slip anchor at Plockton and set sail across Loch Carron for the slightest of that fistful of mingling sea lochs, Loch Toscaig, and Applecross's most endearing flank. Toscaig is where Applecross's other road ends, and from any vantage point above and beyond, the West fans one of its most seductive landscapes at your feet.

The Skye Cuillins inevitably dominate, the way they inevitably do, a fondly formidable profile from anywhere, any distance. The conning tower of Dun Caan on Raasay glows and glowers in wet sun and black shadow, while in mid-Sound, the meek Crowlin Islands re-establish the less romantic side of Gaelic nomenclature. They are Eilean Mor (big island), Eilean Bcag (wcc island) and in between, Eilean Meadhonach (middle island), and presumably Nighean Bhan (Goldilocks) lives here.

Summers on Applecross *can* be idyllic, but the real mesmeric character of the West is unveiled and veiled and unveiled again a dozen times an hour in the rapid-fire sweet-and-sour weather of springs and autumns — big winds, big rains, brief suns, and rainbows as thick on the ground as puddles. Or if Applecross permits it, you may once or twice in a lifetime witness the exquisite snow-powed stillness of a winter storm's morning after, and hold it as a treasure in best Goldilocks fashion, happily ever after. You leave none of Applecross's seasons empty-handed.

Loch Torridon beyond Applecross is not so much a finger of a sea loch as a thing of jaws and a throat. Certainly there are times and landscape moods where your pine-girt progress along the shore of the Upper Loch looks as if it may conclude at any moment with the landscape swallowing you whole.

Irvine Butterfield, author of "The High Mountains of Britain and Ireland", assesses Torridon thus: "Nowhere in Britain do mountains so proclaim their individuality." It is an observation made the more telling in any south-north progression through the West Highlands, for not since the Buachaille and The Ben strutted across those far southern horizons has the power of the West's kingdoms so overwhelmed with the physical presence of individual mountains.

The mountains of Glencoe, Knoydart, Kintail, even skylined Skye, form conspiracies, gathering their landscape strengths from their cheek-by-jowl brotherhoods, submerging individualists. Torridon, by comparison, is a gargantuan contest, its impact on the unwary often an unnerving one. Individually, Beinn Alligin, Liathach, Beinn Dearg (thoughtfully described by Irvine Butterfield as "an unique belvedere"), Beinn Eighe and Slioch would dominate any company. In their own jostling crowd they are a covey of peacocks, outrageous extroverts vying to be seen, or in the worst of the weather, vying to oppress with their massive implications.

Liathach wins it. Nothing, even in this stockpile of sensation-in-stone quite lives up to your first glimpse of that mountain's classic thrust across Loch Clair.

The large-scale maps show Liathach in grotesque swirls, the work of Van Gogh in his wheatfield-with-crows madness, a mapped monster contoured by the crazed cartographers of the Ice. Loch Clair's looking glass calm cannot flatter here, but merely magnifies and mirrors twice the monster. Hamish Brown, in his "Hamish's Mountain Walk", summoned Austrian climber Kurt Diemberger to catch the mood of Liathach: "It is not only the beautiful we seek; the tremendous draws us irresistibly."

It is a good thought for a Torridonian context, not that the place is without beauties, but there is much in that frenetic landmass between Upper Loch Torridon and Loch Maree which is merely "tremendous". Loch Maree itself, however, harbours many beauties, whether you peer down into its long

Facing: **Jostled Beinn Damph** *Above:* **Triumphant Liathach**

A rainbow alights on "that frenetic landmass" above Loch Torridon

sprawl from funnelling Glen Dochertie, or wonder down at it from mighty Slioch (a conning tower to shrivel Dun Caan to a periscope), or ponder across its widest girth at the pine-profusion of its islands.

I have wandered the shoreline pines (envied the mental prospect of a canoe among the islands) one early winter's day here with the music of the car's cassette player still echoing through my mind. It was Solveig's Song from Peer Gynt, and it so caught the landscaped air of Loch Maree that I had to fight back tears. There is music in landscape; there is landscape in music.

These steely gray days of profound calm and shuttered hills have the curious effect of imparting a dark sheen to the pines which I have never been conscious of around the Cairngorms, for example, where the woods sprawl and climb rather than tower, hemmed-in and clinging.

The Caledonian pinewoods are among Torridon's unquestionable beauties, fit drapery for such a rockscape. When you see the rocky odds they overcome to thole life's privilege, you wonder at the meagre extent of the woods, even with the old burnings and the centuries of overgrazing of sheep and deer. So many people agree that the pinewoods should be encouraged, yet so rarely does it happen, and the landscape of the West Highlands is denied the warmth of the great benevolent cloak which once swaddled so much of shores and slopes like these.

You turn north, perhaps reluctantly, for Loch Maree and its pines have assuaged the tremendousness of Torridon with their beauties.

Slioch's conning-tower peers down on pine-girt Loch Maree

Loch Torridon landscapes: Shieldaig headland *(above)* and Beinn-na-h'Eaglaise *(facing)*

"Suilven exerts a presidential presence on its landscape"

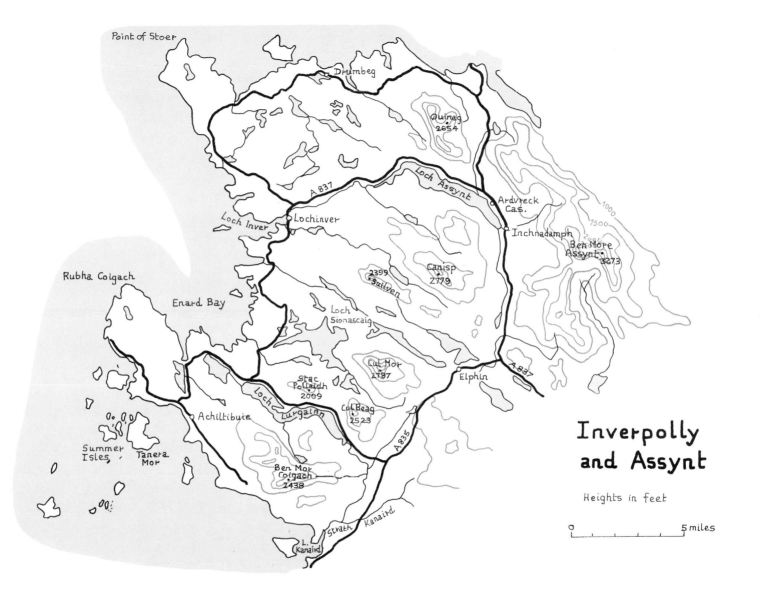

Point of Stoer

Drumbeg

Quinag
2654

Loch Assynt

Ardvreck
Cas.

A 837

Loch Inver

Lochinver

Inchnadamph

1000

1500

2000

Ben More
Assynt
3273

Rubha Coigach

Enard Bay

2399
Suilven

Canisp
2779

Loch
Sionascaig

Cul Mor
2787

A 837

Stac
Pollaidh
2009

Elphin

Achiltibuie

Loch
Lurgainn

Cul Beag
2523

A 835

Summer
Isles

Tanera
Mor

Ben Mor
Coigach
2438

Inverpolly
and Assynt

Heights in feet

0   5 miles

Strath   Kanaird

L.
Kanaird

INVERPOLLY
AND ASSYNT

The coast road north from Loch Maree confronts you with one vivid preview of the nature of the land which beckons. From high above Gruinard Bay a landscape unveils which agriculturally is without a redeeming feature. Geologically, or topographically, or for anyone who holds dear the world's wilder acres, it is a glimpse of Valhalla.

Its coast is shambolic, the great showpiece of the Ice, erratically perforated by that ancient insatiable appetite for lopping off land by the sea-lochful; some mighty bites like Loch Broom, others discreet nibbles of charm and sudden birchwoods like Loch Nedd. Every sea loch and bay and headland is smattered with islands, mostly tiny rock afterthoughts of the land, every one as conspicuous for its bare-boned treelessness as Loch Maree's were for the distinction of their bespoke green garments.

The land seems to hold as much water as rock. A long, lingering study of the large-scale map of, say, the land between Loch Inver and Eddrachillis Bay reveals an area of perhaps 40 square miles and more than 300 lochs and lochans, only a tiny percentage of which the map dares to name. The reality, looking west from Quinag with a low sun raking over the embers of a winter night kindles

Inverpolly profiles: Cul Mor *(facing)*, and Stac Pollaidh *(above)*

"Up here, the Ice was cannier with its mountains than Torridon . . ."

hundreds of new flames on the landscape. It is that kind of land which beckons.

Up here, the Ice was cannier with its mountains than Torridon, accorded each its shuddering upthrust from plinths wild miles wide. You can grin at the audacity of Stac Pollaidh because it is not frowned upon by some green-eyed god-gathering of limelight stealers. It is hardly a beautiful mountain: it is too perpetually dishevelled for that, and from the west, its superstructure is so perilously perched on one flank that the image of an aircraft carrier of obscene dimensions springs to mind. There never was a beautiful aircraft carrier.

A road of sorts hiccups to the sea at Achiltibuie, where for the modest effort of sclaffing up the 500ft of Meall Dearg, you win a spreadeagle of one of the most charismatic island tribes in the West — the Summer Isles. The headland of Rubha Coigeach which accommodates your hill is so deep in the Atlantic that it confers an islander's aspect on the Summer Isles, and throws your mind lurching back to Ardnamurchan with the realisation of how far you have journeyed, and how little you have journeyed. It is a classic symptom of travel in the landscape of the West Highlands.

Anyone who takes a serious inclination to the life and the wildlife and the landscape of the West must — sooner rather than later — encounter the work of Frank Fraser Darling, scientist, naturalist, humanist, conservationist before the word was invented, and one whose insights and perceptions into the problems of living in this

"You can grin at the audacity of Stac Pollaidh . . ."

landscape stamped a convincing authority on everything he wrote. He knew, because he so lived himself. So much of what he wrote was definitive, so much still quoted today as an authority beyond question, particularly on subjects as diverse as red deer, seals, and land use in the Highlands.

Nowhere did he practise what he preached more convincingly than on Tanera Mor, largest of the Summer Isles, and the subject of his book (lamentably long out of print), "Island Farm". While your glasses range across the islands to the massed predatory sharks of the deep sea fishing trade which now flock to Loch Broom, it is worth dwelling on those mariners who once hove to in that still delectable little bay of Tanera Mor called The Anchorage.

"It can be imagined how much used the Anchorage of Tanera would be in the days of sailing boats. Here was one of the safest places on the coast and yet well out to sea. A sailing ship, for example, would not welcome a journey up Loch Broom to Ullapool and out again for the sake of shelter. Ullapool as such did not exist until 1780 or thereabouts, but the Anchorage of Tanera Mor has been busy for a thousand years. The Vikings called the island Hawrarymoir — the island of the haven ..."

Today the Anchorage accommodates a fish farm. That much has changed, but it is still the instinctive choice for those who work the sea in a small way. That much is as it was, and the storms and their suns and their shows of light on the land and the water still rush in from the south-west, still work their magics and their miseries on

The "charismatic tribe" of the Summer Isles

the mainland and its singular mountain profiles. Ullapool fares well on it all — the fishermen, the visitors, and its own small stushie of life as mainland ferry port for the Western Isles and focal point for the sparse humanity of that ancient rock hinterland.

Your journey northwards slips surreptitiously and all but unheralded into Sutherland, to confront you almost at once with the ultimate consummation of that old marriage of Torridonian sandstone and Lewisian gneiss. Suilven is only 2399ft, but it is so sculpted, so enthroned on spaciousness that it exerts a presidential presence on its landscape. And yes, it *is* a beautiful mountain!

Shades of Suilven

Ullapool: ". . . focal point for the sparse humanity of that ancient rock hinterland . . ."

Loch Broom landscapes: Ben Mor Coigach *(above)* and the side-show of Loch Kanaird *(facing)*

Kylesku Bridge: ". . . eloquent concrete in a land of old stone"

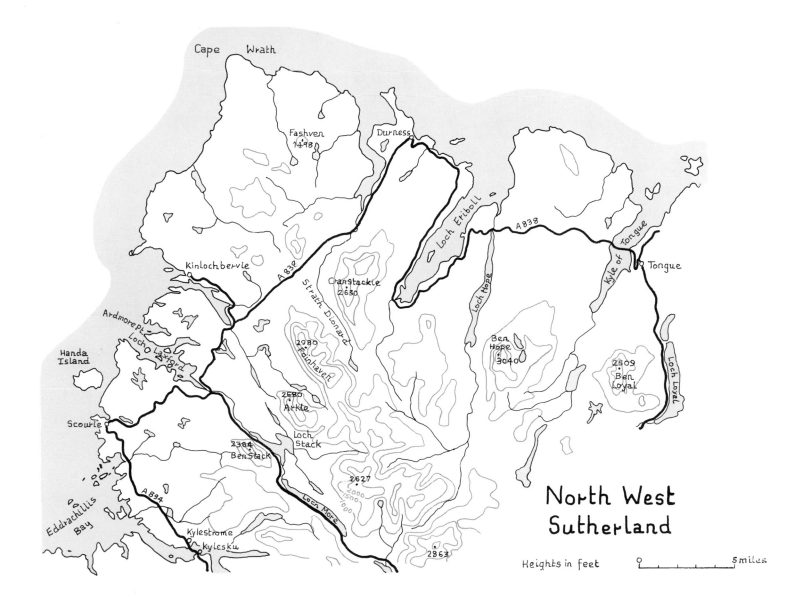

Cape Wrath

Fashven
1498

Durness

Loch Eriboll

A838

Kyle of Tongue

Tongue

Kinlochbervie

A838

Cranstackle
2630

Strath Dionard

Loch Hope

Ben
Hope
3040

Ardmore Pt.

Loch Laxford

2980
Foinhaven

Loch Loyal

2509
Ben
Loyal

Handa
Island

2580
Arkle

Scourie

Loch
Stack

2364
Ben Stack

A894

2627

Loch More

2000
1500
1000

Eddrachillis
Bay

Kylestrome

Kylesku

2863

North West
Sutherland

Heights in feet

0   5 miles

NORTH WEST SUTHERLAND

The traverse of Assynt is no journey for the land-squeamish. It is Scotland's least compromising single malt landscape, untarnished by blending influences, where the unsettling spirit you first encountered on Rannoch Moor finally wins a spectacular unfettered freedom.

At its heart, the mouldering 16th century fortress of the Macleods of Assynt, Ardvreck Castle, succumbs stone by stone to the ways of the wilderness it once dominated. Its vaulted cellars stare blackly out at Quinag which offers in return its most benign — and deceptive — aspect. (Quinag is a chameleon mountain — a two-headed pyramid from Kylesku, a brown "Buachaille" from the Drumbeg road, an unfathomable gray wall from Glen Leireag, a bleak and bloated milestone on days of dark-shuttering cloud.)

Ardvreck's finest hour was the surrender of the military genius, Montrose, who gave himself up here after the Battle of Carbisdale. It would prove the last freely made decision of his life. The Macleod, doubtless inspired by a reward he never won, handed Montrose over to the authorities in Edinburgh where he suffered one of the most celebrated executions in Scottish history.

A raid by Mackenzies accounted for Ardvreck's decline. They put it to fire in 1672, and Sutherland's sea winds and

Quinag *(facing)*: "... a chameleon mountain ...", and Foinaven

69

wearying winters have patiently prized the ruin apart. Ardvreck's situation on Loch Assynt inevitably recalls Eilean Donan on Loch Duich. Its miserable and unexplained condition recalls the Eilean Donan that was, and leaves the traveller yearning for another dreaming clansman whose vision might permit the reassembly of old glories. It is a fine line which distinguishes between thoughtful restoration and meddling with history. Eilean Donan Castle is a persuasive enough ambassador for the former, persuasive enough to argue the case for a born-again Ardvreck.

That way of life, with Gaelic conversation coursing through all this landscape's glens and a castle for a community centre is barely credible now as you thread the new road north through people-starved landscapes towards Kylesku. The Kylesku Bridge has fast won for itself an international acclaim, an eloquent expression of what man can achieve with concrete in a land of old stone. It is a handsome, low profile thing, whose attitudes could have been applied to telling effect elsewhere — say at Ballachulish for example. What it has also achieved however, is to create the opportunity for speed in a landscape cut out for the dawdlers of the world, and there is not much you can do for ferry villages like Kylesku and Kylestrome when the ferry stops sailing. These were consigned at a stroke from mainstream to backwater; the mainstream simply flows overhead, but the story of Sutherland is well punctuated with regimes which marched their own definition of progress across the landscape leaving communities to adjust or adjourn elsewhere.

Norman MacCaig, sublime poet of this landscape found a voice for them in the concluding lines of his long poem "A Man of Assynt":

. . ..And the mind
behind the eye, within the passion,
remembers with certainty that the tide will return
and thinks, with hope, that that other ebb,
that sad withdrawal of people, may, too,
reverse itself and flood
the bays and sheltered glens
with new generations replenishing the land
with its richest of riches and coming, at last,
into their own again.

The tide that lolls in Loch Laxford on a still blue day of early June has filled the rocks to the brim, and having filled, lies slack and exhausted. On such a day, a small boat might put out from Foindle for the purpose of rummaging round the islands and skerries which populate the loch and harbour furtive riches of wildlife.

It isn't all furtive — serried shag sentries line the ledges with uncanny silhouettes, stepping off only when the boat glides a dozen yards by, and snaps their resolve. Tysties and red-throated divers slip quietly under the boat, or paddle energetically away from her bow-wave with one eye cocked over a shoulder, and once, an otter, crab-jawed, creeps ashore on Eilean an Eireannach.

A puzzle resolved here, too, for the bays have herons like Torridon in August has midges, and I had already fallen to

"Characteristically sentinel one-off mountains sit pyramid bold . . ."

Arkle, a classic Sutherland "set piece"

wondering how you construct a heronry in a treeless landscape. The answer is that they cliff-nest on the greening landward steps of Loch Laxford's remoter islets. The boat accords them a respectful berth, for heronries are fractious fickle places at the best of well-treed times, and Loch Laxford is hardly one of these.

Cormorants, true sea beasts, nest on the seaward side, scorning every shred of the loch's countless windbreaks. Beyond Ardmore Point the boat begins to dance to the ocean's tune, the horizon wavers and gannets crash dive the shoals. The world was never bluer than this, the West Highlands never more seductive.

The homeward journey, inspected by ledgefuls of seals, unfolds the great seaward wall of Arkle. It occurs then that Quinag has one just like it. So has Foinaven, and Cranstackie across Strath Dionard, and lonely Fashven up by Cape Wrath. Some semblance of understanding begins to dawn then about the mighty nature of those slow rivers of that lost northern continent of the ancients which fashioned this land. Forces capable of fundamental creations were at work, the landscape you find now a well-worn and dwindled relic of its astounding legacy.

Ben Stack is the workmanship of a subtler sculptor, its classical peak the mountain perfectionist's antidote to Arkle's wall. Its slender summit path is an unexpected airy exhilaration. The summit itself fulfils Beinn Dearg's Torridon role, belvedere to Sutherland's famed set pieces.

According to Sutherland's rarefied definition of the landscape, the West Highlands straggle away eastwards too,

Ben Stack: ". . . workmanship of a subtler sculptor . . ."

73

where characteristically sentinel one-off mountains sit pyramid-bold amid their wide square miles of diver lochs and plover moors and rain-sheened rock. Ben Hope, the highest of these, and the first and last Munro in the land, may be rooted firmly in Sutherland, but seems to dream restlessly out at these immense island-strewn seascapes which its northern ridge unfolds. A roadside sign, "Ben Hope Way Up", has always seemed more suggestive than instructive, hinting at a character assessment of the mountain. Ben Hope always looks way, way up, inclining perpetually northwards, straining at its mainland anchor,
a fey place.

A final eastward lurch of Sutherland's redefined West Highlands permits the infiltration of Ben Loyal. It is a distinguished outpost, for if any single mountain can lay claim to the title of Sutherland's masterpiece, it is surely this one. Your preoccupation is not the view beyond, always the mountain itself, a self-contained alpine world, a pleated, handsome isolationist. It recalls Kintail's sisters transported out into the heart of Rannoch Moor. In the Belvedere, the Dreamer and the Masterpiece, Sutherland seals the landscape fate of the West Highlands with a signed flourish. Only the North Coast urges you on now, demands of you a long lingering look over your shoulder, a speculative glance across a shoreline which for once compels you not west, but irrevocably north.

Ben Loyal: ". . . a pleated, handsome isolationist"

A DIFFERENT LAND

There is a shelf of turf, a headland or so west of Smoo on Sutherland's north shore.

A quarter of a mile of the whitest sand you ever saw that wasn't snow paves the rim of the bay.

The turf is wide enough for a tent, a haflin burn provides water enough for one coffee pot, one toothbrush.

The shore speaks of Maxwell's Camusfearna, but it is no Skye of Gaeldom which lies beyond but Orkney, which is a different kingdom.

I find in this first and last gesture of the West Highland landscape a small encapsulation of all of it — its encroaching seas, its wave-butting rock, its storms, its sanctuaries, its eagle hill, its deer forest, its tree desert, its people echoes, its otter discretion, and all their fragrances.

All these gather here, but the north wind also dusts the place with other scents, the moon is hugely risen over other times and tides.

It *is* a different land beyond Rannoch. It is a different land again beyond Sutherland.

"It is a different land beyond Rannoch . . ."

". . . a different land again beyond Sutherland"